T0244787

Poems from the Soul

Poems from the Soul

M. WYNN THOMAS

Illustrations by Ruth Jên Evans

2024

www.uwp.co.uk

British Library CIP Data

A catalogue record for this book
is available from the British Library.

ISBN: 978-1-83760-011-3

The publisher acknowledges the financial
support of the Books Council of Wales

Printed and bound by CPI Group (UK) Ltd,
Croydon CR0 4YY

FSC
www.fsc.org
MIX
Paper | Supporting
responsible forestry
FSC® C171272

er cof am mam a 'nhad
ac am Graham Rees (1944–2022)

'So, altogether, I am grateful to
my "Congregational" upbringing.
The Congregationalists are the
oldest Nonconformists.'
D. H. Lawrence

Contents

Prefatory Note

Nineteenth-century Wales was 'chapel blest and Bible haunted'. A century later, R. S. Thomas imagined it to have been a period when a preacher could catch fire, and 'burn steadily' before his congregation 'with a strange light'. Yet by his time chapels had come to seem like sinister encumbrances on the Welsh landscape. They were dark, they were 'squat as toads', and 'they raised their faces stonily'.

Giants of the pulpit in that distant Wales of yesteryear were the pop icons of their day. Image-conscious poster boys of their faith, they had special studio photos taken, and these were proudly displayed on the walls of homes and of vestries. Colourful stories about their extraordinary exploits avidly circulated. They even had their groupies – some of the most prominent were trailed from chapel to chapel by their awestruck admirers. And they had their distinctive acts and cultivated images.

In that age of the colossi, Christmas Evans could populate the air with characters and fill it with voices. John Elias could famously galvanise a congregation by conjuring up an auction of souls. His rapt listeners distinctly heard the Devil whispering 'Strike them down to me. I am ready to take them.' The auctioneer, gavel raised, was on the point of clinching the deal. Then a quiet voice was heard: 'I will take them: I will take them as they are to wash in my own blood.' Rabble-rousing maybe. But great spiritual theatre.

Late in the nineteenth century, the loveable redneck, Edward Matthews, Ewenni, was renowned for 'tearing up a Bible during the sermon, bending backwards over the edge of the pulpit, or pulling his coat tails over his head like a hood'. One religious periodical even invited its readers to select their five favourite preachers, and offered a £5 prize to anyone who correctly guessed the top of the pops. And there was delicious rivalry on display too. On one occasion the famous John Elias repeatedly found his sermons interrupted at their crucial climax by the strategically timed coughs of one of his rivals in the preaching stakes.

Many of the hymns collected here emerged out of that background. Some, however, date back to the late eighteenth century, and others belong to the twentieth. There are those in the modern world of the West who seem to believe it has advanced beyond the era of hymns.

'Progress' has outgrown them; 'science' has seen them off. And yet ... they persist in hanging around, evidence of the sense people once made of their world, and testimony to needs that can still suddenly strike one as unnervingly like one's own. They keep cropping up at weddings and funerals, at rugby matches and in pubs. They're to be heard at disasters. In England, one is sung every year, even if without much spirit or conviction, at Wembley before the FA Cup Final. They just refuse to be silenced.

In 1926, D. H. Lawrence – surely one of the least likely of champions of their seemingly lost cause – wrote an autobiographical essay. In it he admitted his own deep indebtedness to the hymns he'd heard sung in chapel when he was a boy – a chapel 'which was tall and full of light, yet still'. It was, he said, 'almost shameful to confess' how much these poems still meant to him. But he remained moved by the evidence he found in them of 'wonder', 'the most precious element in life'. Hymns, he stated, 'live and glisten in a [person's] consciousness in undimmed wonder'.

For me, the hymns of Wales are indeed a wonder. Through them I experience the raw needs of ordinary human experience – needs I recognise as also being my own. They are also powerful social connectives. It is moving to recall that these hymns sustained so many of the Welsh troops doomed to service in the trenches in the First World War. In them, a people voice their hopes and their anguish, their joy and their pain. They are not the products of an intellectual class, nor even of an educated bourgeoisie. They are mostly the spontaneous utterances of farmers and miners, of tinplate workers and blacksmiths. At least one may have been composed orally while milking; another composed, again orally, while tramping the green desert uplands of mid Wales; and yet another was composed in the white heat of a blacksmith's forge.

And in each and every hymn a single, singular voice sings out, loud and strong with fear, with hope, with ecstasy, with anxiety. The following, for example, is the signature voice of William Williams Pantycelyn:

> I peer o'er the distant hills
> in anxious search for you;
> Come, my beloved, it grows late
> and my sun's setting too.

And here is the voice of Mary Owen, a Swansea woman whose entire life is lost in obscurity but who nevertheless lives on in these vibrant lines:

> Here is love beyond expression,
> comprehension it leaves dumb.

The celebrated African American singer and activist, Paul Robeson, was right to recognise in hymns such as this the Spirituals and Gospel Songs of the Welsh people. As a guest at the National Eisteddfod in 1958 he chose a Welsh hymn book as a gift. But can these hymns, made of the stuff of the Welsh language, retain their power when rendered into English? Inevitably not. Particularly when the translating is undertaken by one who has no claim to be a poet.

And then there is the absence from modern English of an equivalent for the word 'ti', which is ubiquitous in these Welsh hymns. Yes, of course, there is 'thou'; but that is a hoary anachronism that can reach us only down the long echoing corridors that divide us from a remote yesteryear. Whereas in modern Welsh 'ti (ti/di)' is the most disarmingly intimate of terms. It is to be used only for immediate family and with the closest of friends. It is also invariably the term of any address to God.

And yet … despite all these obstacles to translation, so compelling is the voicing of universal experience in these hymns, however unfamiliar their rich figurative language, that, surely, something of their urgency can still survive transmission even through a medium that is foreign to their own natural idiom? Even though the best I can manage are no more than crude approximations and rough versifications of the originals?

Does one need to be a 'person of faith' to appreciate these poems? Definitely not. If the biblical language they use, the terms upon which they rely, the 'mythology' on which they draw, can seem unsatisfactory (perhaps even repugnant) to us, then we might do well to remember the sage remarks of the eminent American novelist, Marilynne Robinson. She has in mind particularly the so-called 'Pilgrim Fathers' of her country's Puritan past. 'I have thought about that very often – how the times change, and the same words that carry a good many people into the howling wilderness in one generation are irksome or meaningless in the next.'

These are very much a people's poems – in two senses of that phrase. First, they arose from the ordinary people. The hymns they produced provided them with a welcome new sense of their own importance – of the vital consequence of their humble humdrum lives. These songs, inspired and inspiring, supplied them with a revolutionary new awareness of their central place in the world. They were the compass that allowed them to find their bearings anew.

And secondly, these hymns were a people's poems because they played a vital role – as hymns never did in England – in the creation of a modern people: the Welsh people. By the middle of the nineteenth century the entire country of Wales seemed to be participating in one great Cymanfa Ganu – one great festival of congregational hymn singing. The language of the hymns was a common language; a language that the whole of a new Wales knew by heart.

There was, then, a time, not long distant, when ordinary people in Wales lived the life of which these hymns so eloquently speak. It was a time of faith, at once narrow and intense, when believers 'sang their amens / fiercely, narrow but saved / in a way that men are not now'. Or so R. S. Thomas uneasily claimed. He was partly right. Right that their lives revolved around the fraught issue of salvation. Wrong in supposing that they were enviably certain of being saved. Far from it. The very opposite was in fact true. Calvinism taught that no individual could be certain of being the privileged recipient of God's grace.

Underlying most of these hymns, even at their most confidently assertive, there lurks the anguish of eternal uncertainty, and this lends edge and the power of urgency to their utterances.

How fraught these hymns are may be very difficult for us today to register. This is neatly illustrated by a common misreading of familiar lines from the most famous hymn of them all: 'Guide me O Thou great Jehovah'. 'When I tread the verge of Jordan, / bid my anxious fears subside.' Nowadays this is usually understood to refer to the ordinary, widespread human fear of death. But that is not what its author, William Williams Pantycelyn, fears. His fear is that he may not actually reach the far shore of Canaan, that his soul may perish on the way. Because the crossing of the Jordan is very different from the crossing of the Styx in ancient times. Safe passage across that dark river was guaranteed, whereas for Pantycelyn there could be no certainty that he would ever be allowed to cross the river Jordan in safety and admitted to the Promised Land. Only by the grace of God could he make it to that far shore, and divine grace was wholly unpredictable, and even seemingly fickle, from a human perspective. Those 'songs of praises' that Pantycelyn dreams of one day singing to all eternity will therefore be songs energised by the most immense relief.

That brings us to a central paradox. These hymns are nowadays cherished for their power to voice the passions of a collective. They are the very stuff of which community hymn singing is made. Yet, each hymn speaks of isolation

– the isolation of the individual soul face to face with God. In each one a great drama is staged – the life-and-death struggle between grace and sin that is daily being enacted in the theatre of the solitary self.

These hymns were mostly born of circumstances that were testing. That time is past. There is no reason to mourn its passing, but there is reason, it seems to me, to respect what once was best in the lives of a people renowned, in the nineteenth century, for being a 'people of the chapel'. The hymns provide us with an unparalleled insight into the lives they lived and the belief that sustained them. They are all, in R. S. Thomas's fine phrase, 'laboratories of the spirit'. And the experiments in living that were there conducted remain relevant to us today.

M. Wynn Thomas

Dyma gariad
fel y moroedd

(Here is love that's vast as oceans)

Dyma gariad
fel y moroedd

(Here is love that's vast as oceans)

Dyma gariad fel y moroedd,
  tosturiaethau fel y lli:
T'wysog bywyd pur yn marw,
  marw i brynu'n bywyd ni.
Pwy all beidio â chofio amdano?
  Pwy all beidio â thraethu'i glod?
Dyma gariad nad â'n angof
  tra bo nefoedd wen yn bod.

Ar Galfaria yr ymrwygodd
  holl ffynhonnau'r dyfnder mawr,
torrodd holl argaeau'r nefoedd
  oedd yn gyfan hyd yn awr:
Gras a chariad megis dilyw
  yn ymdywallt yma 'nghyd,
a chyfiawnder pur a heddwch
  yn cusanu euog fyd.

Here is love that's vast as oceans,
  and compassion deep as floods:
Life's unblemished prince is slaughtered,
  slain to save our worthless blood.
Who can fail to love his mem'ry?
  Who can fail to sing his praise?
Here is love that will not perish
  while both heaven and earth remain.

On Golgotha's hill there ruptured
  all the fountains of the deep,
and heaven's dams that were unbroken
  cracked and spilled their waters meek.
Love and Grace abounding mingled
  poured their bounty without stint,
and pure justice twined with mercy
  kissed existence steeped in guilt.

If the stellar preachers of nineteenth-century Wales happened to be writers of songs (hymns), their work could be adoringly sung by large audiences (congregations). And, like today's pop stars, they adopted fancy names that signalled that they no longer belonged to the ordinary run of mortals. Gwilym Hiraethog's 'real' name was William Rees (1802–83). A prominent journalist, and writer, he was adored by the progressive, radical wing of chapel culture for his fierce campaigning on behalf of freedom of several kinds: freedom from the evils of slavery, freedom for the subject peoples of Europe – he corresponded with Garibaldi, one of the creators of the Italian nation, and he staunchly supported Kossuth, Hungary's famous freedom-fighter. Over thirty years a minister in Liverpool, he preached and wrote like a tornado.

As for his hymn, I would argue that it is the greatest of them all because of its extraordinary vision of God as the source of reckless, boundless, unconditional love. It is the great, love-flooded, hymn of Welsh Nonconformity. Central to it is its visionary cosmology. The first verse is fairly nondescript in imagery – to imagine God as oceanic in His mercy is hardly novel – except for the sheer rhythmic urgency of its utterance. It is really a prelude, in which the imagery of water that governs the whole hymn, is arrestingly introduced.

The second verse, however, is written in an entirely different key, that of an apocalyptic vision not of the Day of Judgement, but of the Day of Mercy, Compassion and unstinting Love. Here the compressions of expression become explosive. On Calvary, the pent-up fountains of the deep tear themselves open in eruptive gushers. Spontaneously yielding to the pressure of divine love, heaven's mighty damns 'ymdywallt' (outpour themselves), sending waters cascading with impulsive, unstinting generosity onto parched human soil. Buoyed on this torrent, Hiraethog's lines climax in an erotic vision, the epithalamium of a salvatory marriage: 'a chyfiawnder pur a heddwch / yn cusanu euog fyd'. There could be a reference here to the treacherous embrace of Judas, the disciple who betrays Christ to the Roman soldiers by a kiss, a kiss that is here reversed as pure justice and peace fuse in a rapturous kissing of a guilty world. But the primary reference is to Psalm 85: 10. 'Steadfast love and faithfulness meet: righteousness and peace kiss each other.'

No wonder this spiritually sensuous hymn became known as the 'love song' of the convulsive Welsh religious revival of 1904–5. No religious culture capable of producing 'Dyma gariad fel y moroedd' could possibly be all bad. A hymn to die for, it is also a hymn to live by. And behind it lies a striking story.

Hiraethog had been brought up in the Welsh Methodist faith, the backbone of which was an iron Calvinism unbending in the moral and spiritual requirements it made of its members. But he left the church to join the Annibynwyr, the Welsh equivalent of the English Independents or Congregationalists, a much older Dissenting sect that was traditionally more relaxed and liberal and forgiving in its theology. Why?

Because of what happened to a friend of his who broke the chilly High Calvinist rule governing Sabbath behaviour. And his crime? Instead of attending service, he had walked home on a Sunday to visit his wife who was dangerously ill. His punishment? Peremptory expulsion from his chapel. Hiraethog left with him. And in 'dyma gariad' he transformed the anger and outrage he had felt into an irresistible declamation of the 'alternative' faith he had embraced; one at whose centre lay mercy and love, not justice and punishment. It is Hiraethog's impassioned rejection of the theology, and the cosmology, of a punitive God.

The hymn tune 'Pennant', to which the hymn is usually sung, is a tonal masterpiece of assured strength and thus perfectly suited to the supremely confident vision of divine love that informs the text. Particularly powerful is the downward-stepping bass-line of the tune's opening bars that suggests the unfathomable depths of the oceanic love that is being celebrated. Its composer was T. Osborne Roberts (1879–1948), a native of the border regions of north-east Wales. Originally trained as assistant to the agent of Chirk Castle Estate, he abandoned his profession and devoted himself entirely to music, serving as organist and choirmaster of several chapels.

Mae bod yn fyw
o fawr ryfeddod

(To be alive is sheer wonder)

Mae bod yn fyw o fawr ryfeddod

(*To be alive is sheer wonder*)

Mae bod yn fyw o fawr ryfeddod
   o fewn ffwrneisiau sydd mor boeth,
ond mwy rhyfedd, wedi 'mhrofi,
   y dof i'r canol fel aur coeth;
amser cannu, diwrnod nithio,
   eto'n dawel, heb ddim braw,
y Gŵr a fydd i mi'n ymguddfa
   y sydd â'r wyntyll yn ei law.

Blin yw 'mywyd gan elynion,
   am eu bod yn amal iawn;
fy amgylchu maent fel gwenyn
   o foreddydd hyd brynhawn;
a'r rhai o'm tu fy hun yn benna',
   yn blaenori uffernol gad,
trwy gymorth gras yr wyf am bara,
   i ryfela hyd at wa'd.

To be alive is sheer wonder
   in midst of furnaces so hot.
More strange yet, when I am tempered,
   to be to gold refined my lot.
Day of bleaching, day of winnow,
   all so quiet, without quail,
for He who soon will be my shelter
   is He who now does wield the flail.

Plagued my life by cruel foemen,
   ruthless in pursuit of me;
swarm around me thick as insects,
   noon to night I cannot flee.
Those on my side are most pressing,
   lead the hordes in hellish spree.
But I'll survive by grace's favour
   and keep fighting till I'm free.

Ann Griffiths (1776–1805): the divine Ann: the farm girl of Dolwar Fach. Her story has long been simplified into legend. It is structured around a simple, stark contrast: the young Ann Thomas, a gay, heedless farm girl, fond of songs, dances and revelry; the mature Ann Griffiths, transfixed by conversion in 1796 at the age of twenty, transfigured into the bride of Christ, ecstatic with wonder. This new Ann then flame-fruited into extraordinary eloquence, as the poet Bobi Jones put it. Nor is the legend without its pathetic conclusion. Having married, she gave birth to a little girl, who sadly died a fortnight later. Ann herself followed shortly after. She was just twenty-nine.

As for the hymns by which she became so well known, they were never 'composed' in any formal sense. They were simply spontaneous improvisations, spur-of-the moment effusions, deeply inward and contemplative in character. Ann herself never bothered to write them down (except for one, that survives in her own hand). That they've survived is a miracle in itself. A maid who helped her with the milking was so struck that she committed them to memory, and they eventually made their way to paper. They have about them a visionary intensity akin to that found only in the writings of some of the greatest Christian mystics.

Even though this is one of her simpler poems, its opening lines seem to radiate the fierce heat of her remarkable faith. She has first in mind the churning furnace of ordinary, all-consuming human passions, but hidden within that image is an implicit reference to the famous episode in the Book of Daniel. Three young Jews, Shadrach, Meshach and Abednego, were thrown into a burning, fiery furnace by King Nebuchadnezzar II, king of Babylon, for refusing to bow down before his image. So hot was it that the soldiers who threw them in were all burned, yet the three young Jews miraculously survived totally unscathed – the astonished and awestruck king even claiming that he had seen a fourth man by their side supporting them in the very heart of the flames.

For Ann Griffiths, who knew her Bible inside out, this story perfectly mirrored her own condition, as one who refused to obey the ordinary rules of the world. But to the original Old Testament account she adds a significant twist, because she has the advantage over the original Jewish writers in that she has access to the grace that Christ alone can offer. And so, for her the furnace becomes the furnace of grace, in which the human soul undergoes the spiritual trial and eventual purification attendant upon the workings of divine mercy. And that fourth figure, of course, is the figure of Christ.

But then she switches to other metaphors to describe this condition, and these are drawn directly from her own local farming background – a fine example of the way in which she regularly fused biblical language with terms and images drawn from her own domestic circumstances and experiences. The working of grace is now likened to the process of whitening cloth and then to the labour of separating the grain from the chaff before a wholesome loaf of bread can be baked. And alongside these homely images another also surfaces, this time a much more rare and precious one, befitting the condition of a human soul undergoing purification before being shaped and burnished into gleaming brilliance.

R. S. Thomas, the supreme religious poet of our day, devoted several poems of tribute to Ann's uncanny genius. In one, he recalled how for her 'God [was] in the throat of a bird: Ann heard him speak' – a recognition of the extraordinary ordinariness of her visions. She was his polar opposite in one crucial respect. She seemed to have ready access to spiritual certainty. He, a reluctant child of an age of scientific unbelief, was tormented all his life by spiritual uncertainties. But in another sense they were kindred spirits, spiritual twins, as he intimated by imagining her as 'the figure-head of a ship / Outward bound'. They were both of them voyagers through strange seas of thought alone, bound they knew not where.

The private, singularly confessional, timbre of this hymn finds its musical match in the tune 'Esther,' by the minister known as Ieuan Gwyllt (John Roberts, 1822-77). His *Llyfr Tonau Cynulleidfaol (Book of Congregational Tunes)* ushered in a golden age of hymn singing in late Victorian Wales.

Er mai cwbwl groes i natur

(Although contrary to nature)

Er mai cwbwl groes i natur

(Although contrary to nature)

Er mai cwbwl groes i natur
   yw fy llwybyr yn y byd,
ei deithio wnaf, a hynny'n dawel,
   yng ngwerthfawr wedd dy ŵyneb-pryd;
wrth godi'r groes, ei chyfri'n goron,
   mewn gorthrymderau, llawen fyw,
ffordd yn union, er mor ddyrys,
   i ddinas gyfaneddol yw.

Ffordd a'i henw yn 'Rhyfeddol',
   hen, a heb heneiddio, yw;
ffordd heb ddechrau, eto'n newydd,
   ffordd yn gwneud y meirw'n fyw;
ffordd i ennill ei thrafaelwyr,
   ffordd yn Briod, ffordd yn Ben,
ffordd gysegrwyd, af ar hyd-ddi
   i orffwys ynddi draw i'r llen.

Ffordd na chenfydd llygad barcut
   er ei bod fel hanner dydd,
ffordd ddisathar, anweledig,
   i bawb ond perchenogion ffydd;
ffordd i gyfiawnhau'r annuwiol,
   ffordd i godi'r meirw'n fyw,
ffordd gyfreithlon i droseddwyr
   i hedd a ffafor gyda Duw.

Although contrary to nature
   is my pathway through the world,
I shall travel, in contentment,
   sustained by your face and word;
lift the cross, count it an honour,
   live through trials and not complain,
straight the path, even though bewild'ring,
   till great city home I gain.

Known that path by the name 'Wondrous',
   old, not aged, is this way;
never opened, now beginning,
   path that wakes the dead to day;
way that woos the weary trav'ler,
   way that's Bride and also Head,
way that's sanctified I'll travel
   to rest eternal I am led.

Path no kite's eye ever spotted,
   though it is as plain as day,
path untrod and undetected
   save by faith who knows the Way;
the godless this path leads to mercy,
   the dead it raises to new life,
to criminals it offers pardon,
   peace and favour in God's sight.

Odd: peculiar: a killjoy; and a spoilsport. After her
conversion, Ann Griffith was very aware of being so
regarded by her former friends and acquaintances, who
still mourned the disappearance of the infectious gaiety
and sociability of her old self. And something of the
resultant sense of loneliness seeps into the defiance of
the arresting lines with which her powerful hymn opens.
But after that, it slowly blossoms into ecstatic exaltation
as she gives voice to the far greater joy she has come to
know following her sudden and dramatic conversion.

At the centre of the hymn lies a familiar image of
'The Way' that alone can lead to eternal life. In Ann's day,
pathways were no more than roughly beaten tracks, with
obstacles aplenty. And you had to be certain of your way
– there were few signposts or other aids to safe direction.
To be accompanied by a Guide familiar with the territory
was a great advantage, and in this hymn Christ Himself
is imagined as performing this service.

The strict metre poetry of Wales had always excelled
at definition by multiplying conceits – a form of riddling
known as 'dyfalu'. And this poem offers us a striking
example of how this ancient device, perfected as it had
been in an age when poetry had been caviar for a privileged
few, had by Ann's day come to be adopted and expertly
practised by the ordinary, humble folk of Wales. So Ann
improvises a riff that emphasises the multifaceted and
mysteriously paradoxical features of the way to Salvation
disclosed only by divine grace. Her dexterity in using
verse forms owed something to the tradition of writing

poetry that ran in her family.

Particularly striking is that homely image, drawn directly from her rural experience, of a path that not even the sharp eyes of a red kite, a notorious detector of carrion from afar, could ever hope to detect. The use of the familiar colloquial word 'ffafor'/'favour' (already to be found in the first Bible published in Welsh as early as 1588) is an example of her instinct for domesticating the mysterious world of the spirit without in any way cheapening it in the process. The main characteristic of her hymns is the uncanny ease with which they casually introduce the spiritually arcane into the most ordinary of surroundings, without any jarring changes of register. It is compelling testimony that she is speaking directly from the vividly lived personal experience of a farm girl of very rare spiritual gifts.

As has already been noted, so distinctively personal are Ann Griffiths's hymns as to seem resistant to public, collective expression. It was not therefore until well over a century after her death that this hymn found tolerable musical expression in 'John', the work of E. T. Davies (1878–1969), a professional musician from Merthyr. And this serviceable combination – with Davies opting for a conventional doleful setting in a minor key – has never really found widespread favour with chapel congregations.

Guide me,
O Thou great Jehovah

Guide me, O Thou great Jehovah

Guide me, O Thou great Jehovah,
  pilgrim through this barren land;
I am weak, but thou art mighty,
  hold me with thy powerful hand;
    bread of heaven, bread of heaven,
    feed me now and evermore.

Open now the crystal fountain
  whence the healing stream doth flow;
let the fiery cloudy pillar
  lead me all my journey through:
    strong deliverer,
    be thou still my strength and shield.

When I tread the verge of Jordan.
  Bid my anxious fears subside:
death of death, and hell's destruction,
  land me safe on Canaan's side:
    songs of praises,
    I will ever give to thee.

(Verse 1, tr. Peter Williams)

This, some would claim, is the unofficial national anthem of Wales. Without a doubt, it would be sure to top a poll to choose the hymn best suited for any occasion, secular as well as religious. It is sung at the funerals of the mighty and of the lowly, at weddings both gaudy and plain, in raucous pubs and at beery games of international rugby. It has become the rallying call of an entire people, but it also has worldwide charisma.

And to think it was composed on the hoof (or at least on a horse's hooves) by an ordinary man of extraordinary gifts, who spent his entire life tramping the length and breadth of Wales. He himself estimated that he'd covered some 150,000 miles in all – most of it on horseback. Writing to one of his patrons, he dramatically recorded 'roving and rangeing, over the rude mountains and wild precipices of Wales, in search of poor illiterate souls chain'd in the dens of darkness and Infidelity'. Long before roads of the kind we take for granted today existed, he followed folk pathways, well-beaten tracks over bare hills, skirting bogs, crossing fields and fording rivers. He did so in all weathers. He knew, through the tired bones in his constantly travelling body, exactly what it meant to be a lifelong pilgrim. He knew what it was like to feel small and puny in the face of the elements. And he knew the fear of being confronted by a river in full spate.

To the English, he is known by the commonplace name of William Williams (1717–91). But to the Welsh – particularly those who speak his language – he is known simply as Williams Pantycelyn – often shortened to the affectionate 'Pantycelyn'. Because that is the name of the farmhouse, on the outskirts of Llandovery, where he lived after marriage. In centuries to come the cognoscenti were to claim he was the most naturally gifted poet Wales ever produced. He was certainly by far the most astoundingly prolific. In addition to innumerable collections of hymns, he published several long poems of epic length, and a detailed manual for Christian marriage that did not omit the sensual and sexual dimensions of married love.

At their best, his hymns, carefully composed in the idiomatic Welsh of his own locality to appeal to an uneducated congregation, are remarkable for their effortless marriage of the simple to the profound. So assured are they, that one leading Welsh-language poet of the twentieth century dubbed him 'the Troubadour of Heaven'. Not that Pantycelyn himself would ever have thought of himself as a 'poet'. His hymns – spontaneous and impromptu – were intended to serve a purpose, or rather a complex of inter-related purposes: to familiarise a people newly literate and new to the Bible with the crucial basics of the faith that alone could save them; to awaken in them for the first time an awareness of the infinite value of their own humble souls; to arouse their slumbering intelligence and move them to passionately committed belief. In other words, the hymns were, for Pantycelyn, a vital evangelising tool.

The Wales in which Pantycelyn lived after marriage was well on its way to become what in the USA (to which it had strong Evangelical ties) would be termed a 'burnt-over district'; that is, a region that had been set alight by fiery, populist preachers who proclaimed the Gospel with unequalled fervour. Rejecting the tepid religiosity of the established, and increasingly alien, Church of England, these spiritual rebels and renegades burned to inform their listeners of the path they should follow to gain salvation. They were a reforming movement inside the Church, but were viewed with suspicion and distaste by traditionalists. They were dubbed 'Jumpers' by their detractors because they were given to ecstatic cavorting, and 'Methodists' because they made sure their ecstasy was firmly underpinned by a system of meetings designed to discipline and train the spiritual intelligence of believers. And since their teaching threatened to be subversive of the social, as well as religious, order, these rabble-rousers were treated by mainstream, middle-class society as malcontents, wild ecstatics, 'disturbers of the peace'. At the time when it was written, therefore, 'Guide me' was a kind of rebel song, composed by one who was viewed by the religious and social establishment of the day as something of a spiritual outlaw.

One of the first, and most powerful, of these itinerant preachers was Howell Harris, and it was he who converted Pantycelyn when he was still at a young, impressionable age. Later generations were to call the teachings of these evangelists 'Methodism', because although their preaching was highly emotional in character, they took steps to ensure that the enthusiasm they aroused would not prove merely ephemeral by providing it with an organisational structure designed to strengthen it and to ensure its permanence. In this connection, too, Pantycelyn's hymns were intended to play a crucial role: they were a reprise of the 'lessons' in faith that the evangelists had offered. A combination of reason and feeling, they were a perfect fusion. And as they were intended to be sung by congregations, they were also vitally important bonding rituals – a function 'Guide me O Thou Great Jehovah' continues to serve in our very different day.

The spinal cord of the poem is the biblical story of the 40-year journey undertaken by the Israelites, under their leader Moses, out of bondage in Egypt and through the wilderness in search of Canaan. Several of the key episodes en route are featured by Pantycelyn – God marking the way by acting as a pillar of cloud by day and a pillar of fire by night; the 'manna' God miraculously provided every morning that in the hymn becomes the 'bread of heaven'; while Moses's act of striking a rock to call forth water becomes the opening of a 'crystal fountain' of spiritual healing.

As Pantycelyn explained in a preface to one of his many collections, one of the functions of his hymns was to familiarise congregations to which the Bible had for long been a forbiddingly closed book with crucial landmarks for marking their own journey of faith. They were therefore the equivalent, for the Methodists of the late eighteenth century, of the Scriptural wall paintings that had so liberally adorned the walls of churches in the later Middle Ages. Unfortunately in our increasingly secular age these reference-laden images have for many become irritatingly baffling, little more than an incomprehensible foreign jargon. And yet, in their original context, they were charged with an electrifying power and acquired potent intimacy as believers incorporated them into even the most private experiences of their personal lives.

And then there is the tune, unrivalled in majesty, to which the hymn is invariably sung. Known all over the world, 'Cwm Rhondda' is undeniably the superstar of hymn tunes. And its international status is fitting, since it was named (originally simply 'Rhondda') in honour of what at the beginning of the twentieth century was one of the mightiest of all the world's coal-producing areas. Its composer was John Hughes (1873–1932), a composer and an organist. It was intended for a celebration in Capel Rhondda, in Hopkinstown, Pontypridd. And an intriguing feature is that his celebrated tune was not originally intended for 'Guide me, O Thou Great Jehovah'. Rather, it was meant for one of Ann Griffiths's most renowned hymns, 'Wele'n sefyll rhwng y myrtwydd', and for a Welsh-speaking congregation it continues to serve its original purpose.

Anweledig!
’rwy’n dy garu

(Great unseen, how much I love you)

Anweledig!
'rwy'n dy garu
(*Great unseen, how much I love you*)

Anweledig! 'rwy'n dy garu,
  rhyfedd ydyw nerth dy ras:
tynnu f'enaid i mor hyfryd
  o'i bleserau penna' i maes;
gwnaethost fwy mewn un munudyn
  nag a wnaethai'r byd o'r bron
ennill it eisteddfa dawel
  yn y galon garreg hon.

'Chlywodd clust, ni welodd llygad,
  ac ni ddaeth i galon dyn
mo ddychmygu, chwaethach deall,
  natur d'hanfod di dy hun;
eto'r ydwyf yn dy garu'n
  fwy na dim sydd is y rhod,
A thu hwnt i ddim a glywais
  neu a welais eto 'rioed.

Uchder nefoedd yw dy drigfan,
  llawer uwch na meddwl dyn,
minnau mewn iselder daear,
  bechadurus waethaf un;
Eto, nes wyt ti i'm henaid,
  a'th gyfeillach bur sydd fwy
a chan' gwell, pan fyddych bellaf,
  na'u cyfeillach bennaf hwy.

Great unseen, how much I love you,
  very strange the strength of grace
to draw the soul out, ever gently
  from the pleasures now in place.
you've done more in one split second
  than the world entire has done,
earned yourself a quiet corner
  In this stony heart of one.

No ears have heard, no eyes have witnessed,
  no heart imagined, no minds of men
ever fathomed your true being
  that remains still beyond ken.
And yet I love you, beyond reason,
  more than aught that is below,
beyond all that's reached my hearing
  beyond all that round me grows.

Highest heaven is your true dwelling,
  far above the mind of man,
I in lowly earth am grounded,
  sinful creature, the worst one;
yet, far nearer my soul you linger,
  your pure presence closer seems,
and more precious, when you're distant,
  than man's friendship most extreme.

For me, one of the most endearing features of some of the greatest Welsh hymns is their tone of easy familiarity with God. It is a familiarity that is never familiar. Never is God's complete otherness forgotten. Theirs is a warm familiarity tempered by awe and respect. And it stems from grateful recollection of Christ's instruction to humanity to think of God as 'Abba' and to approach Him as a loving Father. This fine hymn by Williams Pantycelyn is a perfect example of that particular, valuable genre.

But even though it seems keyed to gentle love and affection the hymn is grounded in a sense of the Godhead's ultimate 'otherness' to everything that is human. That opening address to the Almighty as the 'great unseen' should not be passed over lightly. Pantycelyn wasn't only a Methodist – while remaining a member of the Church of England – he was a Calvinistic Methodist (the alternative being Wesleyan Methodism). The theology that was the bedrock of his belief was that systematically outlined in the mid-sixteenth century by John Calvin, the stern religious autocrat of Geneva, who stressed that the 'natural' human condition was one of complete and utter sinfulness and depravity. Human beings had absolutely nothing to recommend themselves – unless they had been visited and saved from their sins by the decidedly capricious grace of a totally unpredictable, wholly unknowable God. Over the centuries, the Calvinists built a majestic structure of theology to contain and articulate the subtle complexities of their faith. Sadly, they are today reductively regarded by many as little better than ignorant, reactionary bigots.

The love that is so beautifully and movingly celebrated in this poem, then, is not 'ordinary' human love. It is the love born of a gratitude for having been inexplicably singled out for salvation. It is this love that, understandably, reaches an ecstatic pitch of gratitude in the concluding lines of the hymn. And at this point, Pantycelyn is so consumed by it that he almost becomes a mysterious stranger to himself, unable as he is to account for what has happened to him and for the feelings by which he is now possessed. The conclusion foregrounds the great paradox of Pantycelyn's faith: that he loves beyond all reason, or rather for a reason that he can never really comprehend, and that he loves a being he can never ever really know. It is the most curious imaginable form of intimacy, and yet intimacy it authentically is, as the affectionately familiar tone of the poetry convinces us.

Behind this hymn there seems to lurk the curious ghost of the Courtly Love poems of Elizabethan times. In that poetry, too, the lover is almost self-abasing in an obsession with a beloved who remains forever distant, aloof and unapproachable, let alone untouchable. But of course for Pantycelyn such poetry would have seemed totally profane, whereas his was devotedly sacred. And his apparent 'abasement' is no such thing; rather it is the abandonment of self that is a necessary precondition for a sinful human soul's reconciliation with God.

As for the solid, four-square tune 'Bethany' to which it is usually sung, it is the work of the prolific English composer Henry Smart (1813–79). Such a cross-border link is not inappropriate, given Pantycelyn's interest in international affairs. But, while powerfully effective, the weighty musical tread of the tune prevents it from conveying the extravagant, intemperate passion that is in Pantycelyn's quicksilver words.

Rwy'n edrych
dros y bryniau pell

(I peer o'er the distant hills)

Rwy'n edrych dros y bryniau pell

(*I peer o'er the distant hills*)

Rwy'n edrych dros y bryniau pell
   amdanat bob yr awr;
tyrd, fy Anwylyd, mae'n hwyrhau
   a'm haul bron mynd i lawr.

Tyn fy serchiadau'n gryno iawn
   oddi wrth wrthrychau gau
at yr un gwrthrych ag sydd fyth
   yn ffyddlon yn parhau.

'Does gyflwr dan yr awyr las
   'rwyf ynddo'n chwennych byw,
ond fy hyfrydwch fyth gaiff fod
   o fewn cynteddau 'Nuw.

I peer o'er the distant hills
   in anxious search for you;
come, my beloved, it grows late
   and my sun's setting too.

Wrest my affections wholly clear
   of this world's iron grip,
attach them fast to One alone
   who'll never let them slip.

There's nowhere under bright blue sky
   I'd rather spend my life,
for dwell I will, contentment find,
   in God's halls, free of strife.

This is the most captivating and most affectionate of Pantycelyn's hymns. His persona is that of the impatiently yearning lover, and his imagery is this time taken from the Song of Songs. Although Pantycelyn was ever wary of the dangerous, unfettered power of human sexuality, he was nevertheless a fully sensual man, well capable of appreciating the fulfilment that comes through the disciplined experience of the senses. He was also ready to recognise the affinity between certain forms of erotic and sexual experience. In another of his poems, for example, he writes seductively as follows of his passion for union with Christ: 'Fel pwysi o fyrrh aroglaidd pur, / Ydyw f'anwylyd gwiw; … / A rhwng fy mronnau caiff e' fod, / Trwy gydol faith y nos.' 'My fair beloved is a bundle of sweet-smelling myrrh; … / and betwixt my breasts he shall lie throughout the long hours of night.'

But if the language of the Song of Songs echoes through this hymn, so does the language of a love poetry that was much nearer home for Pantycelyn: the language of Welsh folk songs, known as 'penillion telyn' because they were often sung to harp accompaniment. A common theme in these – as of course in poems far more sophisticated – was that of a lover pining for the beloved, often standing forlorn at some woodland tryst, or perhaps standing beneath her window in hope of gaining admittance. Pantycelyn is relying on familiarity with this kind of poetry when he writes his hymn, because part of its point is that it, too, is a love poem; one that taps into ordinary feeling but does so in order to raise it to an entirely different plane.

As so often in these hymns, the powerful dynamo driving the experience is in fact a longing for security – a longing the depth of which is perfectly understandable given how much more uncertain life would have been for ordinary people in these past times than it is in the countries of today's relatively settled, affluent West. Death in childbirth was all too common; as equally was death in early childhood. There were no defences against disease such as we fortunately have today.

The basics of livelihood were hard come by. Those members of Pantycelyn's congregation who were agricultural labourers would have known all too well what it was like to live from hand to mouth; those who were small tenant farmers would have been aware that they were in increasing danger of being turned out of their farms – the agricultural revolution was already well under way in the countryside. The rural craftsmen, too, could already sense that radical changes lay ahead. When, therefore, Pantycelyn strikes a note of intense personal concern – as he does in the very opening of this poem – he is tapping directly into fears common to all his listeners. And he is expressing his Calvinistic concern of whether the 'beloved' would in fact ever come – and if He did, would He arrive in time? And the climax of the poem is in its rather wistful vision of absolute, unconditional security; the security of relation with the One who is certain to remain ever the same. That, indeed, is paradise – or sublime, everlasting 'contentment', to use the language of the hymn itself.

Given that this hymn opens on widening horizons, it seems appropriate that the tune to which it is usually sung was written by Daniel Protheroe (1866–1934), who early left his Swansea valley home for Scranton, Pennsylvania, where he spent the rest of his life. Entitled 'Hiraeth' (Longing), it nicely captures both Protheroe's earthly homesickness and Pantycelyn's yearning for his transcendent spiritual home.

Dros bechadur
buost farw

(For a sinner were you tortured)

Dros bechadur buost farw
(For a sinner were you tortured)

Dros bechadur buost farw,
    dros bechadur, ar y pren,
y dioddefaist hoelion llymion
    nes it orfod crymu pen;
dwed i mi, ai fi oedd hwnnw
    gofiodd cariad rhad mor fawr –
marw dros un bron â suddo
    yn Gehenna boeth i lawr?

Dwed i mi, a wyt yn maddau
    cwympo ganwaith i'r un bai?
Dwed a ddeui byth i galon
    na all gynnig 'difarhau?
Beth yw pwysau'r beiau mwyaf
    a faddeui? O ba ri'?
Pa un drymaf yw fy mhechod
    ai griddfannau Calfari?

Arglwydd, rhaid i mi gael bywyd;
    Mae fy meiau yn rhy fawr,
fy euogrwydd sy'n cydbwyso
    â mynyddoedd mwya'r llawr:
rhad faddeuant, gwawria bellach,
    gwna garcharor caeth yn rhydd,
fu'n ymdreiglo mewn tywyllwch
    'nawr i weled golau'r dydd.

For a sinner were you tortured,
    for a sinner, on the tree,
you endured the sharp nails' pierce,
    bowed your head, asked no reprieve,
so do tell me was I that one
    you remembered in your pain,
one on very verge of sinking
    in hell's fierce flames profane.

Oh do tell me will you pardon
    repeats many of old faults?
Tell me will you ever visit
    a hard heart without repent?
What's the worst of sins forgiven?
    and of what kind would they be?
And the groans of crucifixion
    could they heaviest of all be?

Life through you I deeply wish for,
    yet my sins are far too great,
and my guilt is far outweighing
    mountains that around me wait.
Ready mercy, do please hurry,
    set a prisoner wholly free,
who's been fumbling in the darkness
    yearning to have glimpse of Thee.

This must be the most anguished of all Welsh hymns. Its agony is naked and palpable. And placed next, as it is here, to the sweet hymn 'I peer over distant hills' it gives us some idea of the staggering scope of Pantycelyn's encounters with his Saviour.

That repetition, in the opening lines, of 'For a sinner' registers his stunned disbelief that Christ could have allowed himself to be killed in order to save him – him, above all others; that he alone could have been responsible for such appalling self-sacrifice. Equally electrifying is his unexpected confession that, in spite of this, he still seems incapable of true repentance, and his desperate attempt to wring out of Christ some indication of the magnitude of the sins He is willing to forgive. As if he is prepared to bargain with Him over the matter.

And then, there's the dramatic juxtaposition at the beginning of the last stanza of two starkly opposed statements: first a tortured demand that he must somehow be given life, immediately followed by a recognition that his sins are so mountainous as to seemingly rule that out entirely. The whole poem is intensely tragic in its import – until, that is, those final lines when he unexpectedly wins through to confident hope, based on his reawakened realisation that Christ's mercy is offered freely even to the worst and most recalcitrant of sinners.

In 1548, Ignatius Loyola, founder of the militant new Society of Jesus (the Jesuits), published a series of spiritual exercises. Their aim was to counter the effects of the Protestant Reformation by deepening the inwardness of individual Catholic experience. And as one of several valuable means to that end, they instructed the believer in how to envisage that they were present at the crucifixion of Christ by employing every one of the senses to bring home the impact of such a shattering experience. Loyola's manual was to have a considerable influence on the arts of that day. Some of the greatest religious poetry of John Donne was modelled on Loyola's method. And Caravaggio was one of several painters of the Renaissance who put Loyola's teachings to dramatic visual effect. This hymn by Pantycelyn may reasonably be described as a Welsh Methodist's answer to Loyola: indisputable evidence that the drama of the crucifixion, and its centrality to the salvation of the individual soul, could be apprehended every bit as profoundly by a Protestant as by a Catholic. In this extraordinary work he conclusively shows himself to be the Caravaggio of Welsh hymn-writers. His hymn is full of verbal and spiritual chiaroscuro, dramatic juxtapositions of hope and despair.

That this is a deeply personal hymn is beyond dispute. On one level, Pantycelyn may well be offering his own dire plight as a test case, framing it as an extreme instance of unworthiness that might help others to surmount their own similar crises of faith. But at another level there can be no doubting that this hymn is a genuine *cri de cœur* of a soul in an agony of deeply human uncertainty as to its eventual fate. No wonder that Pantycelyn has been described as a major Romantic poet. Nothing quite as searingly confessional as this can be found in the work of the greatest of his English Romantic contemporaries.

As for its accompanying tune, 'Nasareth', it is a tour de force, so perfectly is the melody moulded to the shape of the words and emotions. At one point it even approximates to recitative, as it perfectly catches the natural inflection of a desperately impassioned speech: 'Dwed i mi ai fi oedd hwnnw' / 'Oh! do tell me, am I that one'. The composer was J. R. Lewis, who had been so sickly as a boy that he'd received very little education. But since he displayed conspicuous musical talent, Lewis was taken for training by one of the musical luminaries of the Victorian period, and went on to a career as an organist.

Dyma gariad, pwy a'i traetha?

(Here is love beyond expression)

MARY OWEN

Dyma gariad, pwy a'i traetha?

(Here is love beyond expression)

Dyma gariad, pwy a'i traetha?
  Anchwiliadwy ydyw ef;
dyma gariad, i'w ddyfnderoedd
  byth ni threiddia nef y nef;
dyma gariad gwyd fy enaid
  uwch holl bethau gwael y llawr;
dyma gariad wna im ganu
  yn y bythol wynfyd mawr.

Ymlochesaf yn ei glwyfau,
  ymgysgodaf dan ei groes,
ymddigrifaf yn ei gariad –
  cariad mwy na hwn nid oes;
cariad lletach yw na'r moroedd,
  uwch na'r nefoedd hefyd yw:
ymddiriedaf yn dragwyddol
  yn anfeidrol gariad Duw

Here is love beyond expression,
  comprehension it leaves dumb;
here is love, no part of heaven
  ever can its compass run;
here is love leaves soul uplifted
  high above the gifts of earth;
here is love that leaves me singing
  grateful for what heaven gives birth.

I take refuge in his gashes,
  I take shelter 'neath his cross,
I rejoice in his warm loving,
  greatest love that ever was;
wider is this love than oceans,
  higher too than heavens above,
I place all my trust for ever
  in God's endless, boundless love.

The chapels have a bad name for their supposed suppression, and even oppression, of women. But that is rather unfair. After all, the very beliefs on which they were based helped open the door to women. They rejected the traditional ecclesiastical idea of a sacred, anointed, male priesthood, divinely appointed to be interpreters of Scripture and acting as conduits of God's grace to humble lay worshippers. Instead, they believed that every true believer was their own priest, who had no need for an interfering priesthood to lead them directly into the presence of God. For them, the Bible was authority enough. Every believer had access to it, and by reading it and meditating deeply upon its message all believers could enter into the presence of the Almighty. Therefore every believer, female as well as male, could enjoy a unique personal relationship with God himself, and bear public witness to that unique, transfiguring experience – although the chapel patriarchy, it's true, frequently prevented this happening.

The female witness in this particular poem is Mary Owen (1796–1875), a member of a chapel congregation in the Swansea area at the very beginning of the nineteenth century. She lived on the outskirts of a town already beginning to be renowned for its daring seafarers. Swansea was on the cusp of becoming known worldwide as 'Copperopolis', the world's primary centre for the smelting of copper. The town's population had increased by 500 per cent over the previous century, due to the opening of a series of copper works in its hinterland.

And by 1810 Swansea was responsible for producing 60 per cent of the world's copper.

Where Mary Owen lived was ringed by several of the greatest copper-works in the world, and the air was filled with the pungent smell of sulphur. A popular verse of the time ran as follows: 'It came to pass, in days of yore / the Devil chanced upon Landore. / Quoth he, 'By all this fume and stink, / I can't be far from home I think.' A century later, the region of the lower Swansea valley, where she lived, was to gain notoriety as one of the most polluted areas in the UK. Her hymn transforms the Devil's own landscape into a divine vista. Working in that environment was a literally killing experience. The lives of the men were brutally short. Little wonder, then, that Mary Owen yearns in imagination for escape to a far kinder, gentler realm, or that she places a premium on shelter and safety.

Since the local sources of copper had long since been exhausted, the deep-sea sailors of Swansea port had to travel as far as Chile to find the rare ore on which the local metallurgical industries depended. Venturing out in flimsy sailing ships – steam ships entered service somewhat later – they regularly voyaged around Cape Horn, the very roughest of rough passages, and by far the most perilous. No wonder, therefore, that for her concluding, climactic image for the unimaginable immensity of God's love, Owen turns to the vast sea with which the intrepid sailors of Swansea were so bravely familiar. And for its utter, baleful unpredictability she substitutes a vision of an oceanic love forever calm, loving and benign.

Hers is a poem still beloved by chapel-goers of today because it uses the dialect of its locality. The Welsh term used for 'lift up', for example, is 'cwyd' – which when I was a boy growing up in the Swansea area a stone's throw from where Mary Owen lived, was very much the term still used by parents when urging their children to get up off their lazy backsides. And the opening line of the hymn is, in Welsh, arresting in its colloquial simplicity as it challenges anyone to find words adequate to describe the love of God. It is the way in which this homeliness is blended with sublimity that makes this hymn rather special. It is eloquent proof that, at their best, the chapels could enable ordinary people, living ordinary lives, to have truly extraordinary experiences and that moreover they could provide them with a language and opportunity for sharing those precious personal experiences with others.

It has also been fortunate enough to be set to a magnificent modern tune. 'Garthowen' is the work of Wyn Morris (1929–2010), an internationally prominent Welsh conductor with an unenviable reputation for being truculent and abrasive in the grand manner of the pampered classical music 'maestros' of old. In 'Garthowen', however, this autocratic high-handedness is transformed into the grandeur appropriate to the musical expression of the majesty of Mary Owen's confident spiritual vision.

Wrth gofio'i riddfannau'n yr ardd

(His groans I recall, among trees)

THOMAS LEWIS

Wrth gofio'i riddfannau'n yr ardd

(His groans I recall, among trees)

Wrth gofio'i riddfannau'n yr ardd,
   a'i chwys fel defnynnau o waed,
aredig ar gefn oedd mor hardd,
   a'i daro â chleddyf ei Dad,
a'i arwain i Galfari fryn,
   a'i hoelio ar groesbren o'i fodd;
pa dafod all dewi am hyn?
   Pa galon mor galed na thodd?

His groans I recall, among trees,
   his sweat like great droplets of blood,
his ploughed back made ugly by lash,
   the blow struck by Father above,
and then to be Calvary led,
   and nailed from free choice to the tree,
what tongue can cease speaking of this?
   What heart without weeping can be?

The point, and the power, of this hymn is its unusual brevity – a brevity that seems to indicate that these few words say it all. For a believer such as its author, Thomas Lewis (1759–1842), they are the very soul and epicentre of faith. Nothing else needs to be added. To fully comprehend them is to apprehend the strangeness of a perpetually astonishing self-sacrifice. The sentence structure gives the lines a fateful onward momentum – the first sentence doesn't end until the end of the penultimate line. There is an inevitability to it all – at once horrible and, from the author's point of view, sublime. It details the agony of torture, and the poetry itself seems tortured by anguish.

As for the physicality of the hymn, it may disturb the fastidious with its grossness. But remember this: Thomas Lewis was an ordinary blacksmith; he knew what it was like to sweat, to break one's back at hard physical labour, to grunt from the effort of hammering hard, recalcitrant metal into shape. He was the blacksmith at Talyllychau (Talley), a small rural village situated between Llandeilo and Lampeter. On its outskirts stand the remains of Talley Abbey, founded around 1185 by a local warlord, a reminder that this unremarkable little place has long been an important centre of faith.

There is poignancy and point, however, in the striking evidence offered by this hymn that by the nineteenth century the focal point of spirituality in this community – as throughout Wales as a whole – had shifted dramatically. It had taken up a new home in the village forge – the remains of which one can still pass to this very day: it may be found almost directly after passing the village school, which stands immediately at the entrance to Talley as one travels from the direction of Llandeilo. It is a very short distance from there to the abbey, but it is a distance that measures a remarkable journey, a journey to 'domesticate' and 'democratise' faith. It is a journey that was undertaken by the whole of the people of Wales. As Elfed, one of the prominent hymn-writers of a later day defiantly put it, speaking on behalf of all the chapel members of his 'Nonconformist' Wales, 'Nid oes i ni offeiriad ond Iesu Grist ei hun.' 'There is for us no priest save Jesus Christ Himself.'

This, then, is very much a blacksmith's poem, and it is in its way a structure, of language and of faith, that is every bit as majestic as was Talley Abbey in its prime.

And it has also found powerful musical expression through 'Siloh Newydd'. The work of Ivor Owen (1889–1968), it faithfully tracks the contortions of anguished feeling recorded in the words. So the music, too, ebbs and flows until it ends on the appropriate note of calm affirmation.

Calon lân

(A pure heart)

Calon lân
(A pure heart)

Nid wy'n gofyn bywyd moethus,
  aur y byd na'i berlau mân,
gofyn 'rwyf am galon hapus,
  calon onest, calon lân.

    Calon lân yn llawn daioni,
      tecach yw na'r lili dlos;
    dim ond calon lân all ganu,
      canu'r dydd a chanu'r nos.

Pe dymunwn olud bydol
  chwim adenydd ganddo sydd;
golud calon lân, rinweddol
  yn dwyn bythol elw fydd.

    Calon lân yn llawn daioni,
      tecach yw na'r lili dlos;
    dim ond calon lân all ganu,
      canu'r dydd a chanu'r nos.

Hwyr a bore fy nymuniad
  gwyd i'r nef ar adain cân
ar i Dduw, er mwyn fy Ngheidwad,
  roddi imi galon lân.

    Calon lân yn llawn daioni,
      tecach yw na'r lili dlos;
    dim ond calon lân all ganu,
      canu'r dydd a chanu'r nos.

I ask not for sumptuous living,
  pearls and gold, the wealthy's lot,
heart that's pure alone I ask for,
  heart that's honest, without blot.

>   A pure heart that's full of goodness,
>   lovelier far than lily fair,
>   such a heart alone can glory
>   in a song beyond compare.

Had I wished for worldly treasure,
  on swift wing it would away,
wealth of heart that's pure and noble
  earns me profit ever stays.

>   A pure heart that's full of goodness,
>   lovelier than the lily fair,
>   such a heart alone can glory
>   in a song beyond compare.

Late and early my petition,
  raised to heaven on wings of song,
is that God, for sake of Jesus,
  gift me heart that's pure and strong.

>   A pure heart that's full of goodness,
>   lovelier than the lily fair,
>   such a heart alone can glory
>   in a song beyond compare.

Fifty years ago it was worth arriving at the old Cardiff Arms Park well before the game of international rugby was due to begin. Because to while away the hours of waiting, the steadily swelling crowd would sing its way through its repertoire of Welsh hymns. It sang in immaculate four-party harmony, a skill, taught in the Sunday schools of the chapels, that has sadly been lost. And one of the highlights on such occasions was 'Calon Lân'.

Its author was Daniel James (1847–1920), whose highfalutin (bardic) name was 'Gwyrosydd'. Born on the industrial outskirts of Swansea, he lost his father when he was 13, and accordingly started to work at the local tinplate works to support his family. For the rest of his life he worked either in such works or underground. Far from being the model of Victorian probity and respectability that the hymn might suggest, James was very much the local 'bad boy', notorious for his love of drink. He was known to gatecrash weddings, heading for the booze and hoovering it up before the wedding ceremony had even come to an end. His geniality, however, meant that he was very well liked in his native area, and his popularity was no doubt augmented by his talent for slick rhyming – he could produce verses, sentimental, sad or scurrilous, to suit every local occasion.

Given his reputation as an enthusiastic and talented drinker, it is no surprise that the words of this hymn were reportedly scribbled first on a beer mat, at the end of a drinking session at a pub in Blaengarw, an industrial valley within a stone's throw of Swansea where he spent some time working in the local mine.

Colourful reprobate though James may have been, he certainly knew his Bible – as did most of chapel-going Wales during his lifetime. As he would have been fully aware, his hymn is a riff on one of the Beatitudes, the eight sayings of Jesus that were included in the Sermon on the Mount. Calon Lân is an expansion of the sixth of these: 'Blessed are the pure in heart, for they will see God.'

It seems a beautifully simple saying – simple, that is, until one asks the obvious question: 'what did Jesus mean by "pure"'? It is a subject on which the most brilliant theologians have meditated deeply. The Danish existentialist philosopher Søren Kierkegaard, for example, concluded that 'purity of heart ... is a figure that compares the heart to the sea ... for the reason that the depth of the sea determines its purity, and its purity determines its transparency ... so may the heart become pure by yearning only for the good'.

Gwyrosydd, of course, has not the slightest interest in such subtleties of interpretation. A connoisseur of intoxication, he celebrates the greatest intoxication of all; that of singing. Chapel culture in Wales has a baleful reputation for being stern, doleful and joyless. But as this hymn shows, such a reputation is unfair. Gwyrosydd's hymn is an endless celebration of joy – even of ecstasy. In it, purity of heart is associated with a boundless rapture that spontaneously breaks into song. And it offers conclusive proof that a powerful hymn could be written as well by an engaging rogue as by an obedient 'saint'.

Gwyrosydd asked a friend and fellow-worker, John Hughes (1872–1914), to compose a melody for the hymn. Having begun work as an office boy, Hughes ended up as marketing manager, a post that required extensive international travel. To equip himself for the job, he taught himself six languages additional to the two in which he was of course already fluent.

Bracing and buoyant, the tune too is entitled 'Calon Lân'. Particularly thrilling for singers is the trampoline octave jump at the beginning of the chorus: it provides them with exactly the giddy momentum and heady uplift that the words require.

Tydi, a roddaist liw i'r wawr

(O you, who gave to dawn its hue)

Tydi, a roddaist liw i'r wawr

(O you, who gave to dawn its hue)

Tydi, a roddaist liw i'r wawr
   a hud i'r machlud mwyn,
Tydi, a luniaist gerdd a sawr
   y gwanwyn yn y llwyn,
O cadw ni rhag colli'r hud
sydd heddiw'n crwydro drwy'r holl fyd.

Tydi a luniaist gân i'r nant,
   a'i su i'r goedwig werdd,
Tydi, a roist i'r awel dant
   ac i'r ehedydd gerdd,
O cadw ni rhag dyfod dydd
na yrr ein calon gân yn rhydd.

Tydi a glywaist lithriad traed
   ar ffordd Calfaria gynt,
Tydi, a welaist ddafnau gwaed
   y Gŵr ar ddieithr hynt,
O cadw ni rhag dyfod oes
heb goron ddrain na chur na chroes.

O You, who gave to dawn its hue,
   and charm to setting sun,
O You, who fashioned song and scent
   Of springtime bush for everyone,
O do not let the wonder fade
that now is clear in sun and shade.

O You who gave to brook its tune
   and sigh to swaying trees,
O You, who gave to wind its moan
   and skylark's flight its ease,
O save us from a day that brings
a heart so hard it will not sing.

O You who heard the slide of feet
   for Calvary were bound,
O You who saw the bloody drops
   of One whose task astounds,
O save us from an age of gain
that's thornless, with no cross or pain.

This hymn is different from the others in two ways. First, it was written during the 1930s, long after the golden age of the Welsh chapels had come to an end. Secondly, it is the work of a professional writer. Its author, T. Rowland Hughes (1903–49), also published a number of fine Welsh-language novels, genial and popular, about industrial society both in the great quarrying districts of north Wales, his native region (his own father was a quarryman), and in the valleys of the south Wales coalfield, adjacent to Cardiff, where he had briefly taught before finding employment as a producer for the BBC.

However, this hymn also resembles the others in one crucial respect. It is the product of tried and tempered experience – experience that in Hughes's case became about as testing as it comes. In 1937, when he was just 34, he was diagnosed as suffering from multiple sclerosis. Over the following years, he became progressively disabled, but remained in post until 1945. He died just four years later. No wonder that, after his death, one of Wales's most prominent poets was to style him 'the bravest of our authors'.

As if in anticipation of what was to come, his hymn conveys a heightened appetite for ephemeral life and its endless glories. This is the world as seen by a man who knew how the Depression of the 1930s was ravaging the valley communities of contemporary south Wales. It is as if, when viewed across this grim background, the precious fragility of life was almost cruelly foregrounded. So, too, was the hope – or rather, perhaps, the defiantly affirmative belief – that 'a kelson of the creation is love', as the American poet Walt Whitman so memorably put it. In Hughes's case, this belief is grounded in his passionate conviction that God Himself, in the person of Christ, had subjected Himself to the kind of atrocious suffering that was all too frequently the fate of humankind.

The view that Hughes takes of the bloodiness of the crucifixion in this poem is subtle and sophisticated. On one level, he clearly shares the orthodox theology of the Cross, and the belief that a world from which that episode had been erased would be a godless world without the possibility of either meaning or human redemption. But on another level, he's saying something much more arresting, much more original. He is praying that humans should never become so desensitised – by the comforts in which they are cocooned; the hedonism to which they have become addicted – to the reality of suffering that was instanced by the Cross, that they become incapable of that empathy with the afflicted from which alone effective help and support can flow.

Some might say that in parts of today's world – particularly in the affluent countries of Western culture – this possibility seems to loom ominously large. And if anyone had warranty to speak such a warning – who had earned the right to argue a case for pain – it was surely T. Rowland Hughes, in view of the grim suffering he was to endure shortly after composing his hymn.

He also wrote another hymn that is in some ways a pendant to this, a hymn so simple and artless as frequently to be associated with childhood. In it he speaks of a picture he has hanging on the wall next to his bed. It is a popular reproduction of Albrecht Dürer's celebrated chalk drawing of praying hands. And for Hughes, it comes to acquire a totemic value. It is his reassurance that his life is constantly shepherded and guarded by prayer. And his hymn ends by imagining that someday his soul will in its turn undertake that beseeching journey upwards that Dürer's image so movingly represents.

The beloved tune to which the words are set has become a huge favourite of male-voice choirs in Wales, because the volleying cascade of 'Amens' with which it ends (an afterthought of composition) affords them the perfect opportunity to let rip and thoroughly exercise their vocal cords. The piece is the work of Arwel Hughes (1909–86), a figure as well known in the musical world of mid-twentieth-century Wales as was the novelist T. Rowland Hughes in the literary world. Having trained at the Royal College of Music under Ralph Vaughan Williams, he embarked on a long career in the BBC in Wales that culminated with his being appointed head of music, and he was director of music at the investiture of the prince of Wales at Caernarfon in 1969. His son, Owain Arwel Hughes, is an internationally established conductor of classical music.

His tune is noted not least for its sensitive flexibility, which allows it both to express the quiet celebratory affirmations of the hymn's first two gentle stanzas and the darkly intense sobriety of tone of the final stanza.

O Dduw,
a roddaist gynt

(O God, who once did place)

TOMI EVANS

(1905–82)

O Dduw, a roddaist gynt

(O God, who once did place)

O Dduw, a roddaist gynt
    dy nod ar bant a bryn,
a gosod craig ar graig
    dan glo'n y llethrau hyn,
bendithia waith pob saer a fu
yn dwyn ei faen i fur dy dŷ.

Tydi sy'n galw'r pren
    o'r fesen yn ei bryd,
a gwasgu haul a glaw
    canrifoedd ynddo 'nghyd:
O cofia waith y gŵr â'r lli'
a dorrodd bren i'th allor di.

Ti'r hwn sy'n torri'r ffordd
    a'i dangos ymhob oes,
bendithia sêl dy blant
    a'i troediodd dan eu croes;
rho weled gwerth eu haberth hwy
fel na bo glas eu llwybrau mwy.

O God, who once did place
    Your signature on hill and vale,
and set one rock upon the next,
    locked safely into slope and dale,
recall the masons now long gone
who carted stones to build your home.

O You, who call forth growing tree
    from acorn when its season's due,
combining there both sun and rain
    of ages into one green hue,
recall the working man with saw
who shaped the altar's wood with awe.

O You, great navvy, opening roads
    for our own use and gain,
who blessed the zeal of those who walked
    those pathways when in pain;
remind us of their sacrifice
so that their ways may still suffice.

I end with this hymn because it is in one way a summation of the contribution made by ordinary working men and women to our culture through the wealth of powerful hymns they produced out of the often impoverished circumstances of their everyday lives and the stuff of their most intimate experiences. It is arrestingly unusual because it is a tribute not only to the authors of those hymns whose names are known to us but also to the myriad individuals, unknown and forever unknowable, who made vital, undemonstrative contributions to the spiritual life of the Welsh nation. And it makes it clear that, in the end, we are indebted to the anonymous many who have preceded us in their precious, distinctive efforts to make serious sense of their lives. It is a reminder that, in the end, we all live a life in common.

The hymn brings to my mind a fine, witty poem written by the post-war poet John Ormond. As its title, 'The Cathedral Builders', makes clear it features the masons involved in the construction of the majestic edifices of the Middle Ages, 'deifying stone' in the process as Ormond vividly puts it. The poem is unsparing of the gross details of their existence, imagining them as quarrelling and cuffing their children, sweating and spitting, tortured by rheumatism as they aged, and going ever more effortfully and reluctantly to their work. The poem ends with Ormond noticing, with the eye of his imagination, how, when at last their masterpiece was finished, they:

Stood in the crowd
Well back from the vestments at the consecration,
Envied the fat bishop his warm boots,
Cocked up a squint eye and said, 'I bloody did that'.

Quite. Very well said. John Ormond was himself the son of a shoemaker and had a lifelong respect for craftsmen and craftswomen of every kind. And one can likewise imagine some of the writers of these hymns, who were themselves master-builders of sacred language, taking a similarly quiet, unassuming satisfaction in the way that their work continues to offer us today a dwelling-place for our own spirits, be we Christian believers or not.

'Gopsal', the tune to which the hymn is usually sung, is the work of George Frederick Handel no less (1685–1759). Taking its name from a Leicestershire parish and redolent of the hymnody favoured by the Church of England, a hymnody that cannot help but bring to mind public school services, it sounds distinctly odd when sung to Welsh words affirming the humble skills of ordinary people.

Acknowledgements

The staff of the University of Wales Press have been exemplary, as ever, in their meticulous overseeing of the production of this text. My particular thanks in this connection go to Abbie Headon, Amy Feldman and Steven Goundrey. Two very good friends of mine, Professor Stevie Davies and Professor Ceri Davies, both eminent in their respective fields, offered me invaluable advice on the development of the text. But such sweeping statements as I am guilty of should not be charged to their account. This book is dedicated to the memory both of my parents, who, to my everlasting regret, sadly passed away before ever a word of mine had seen print, and of my cousin Graham Rees, a mere month older than I, who passed away in 2022. All three loved the extraordinary hymns of Wales.

The translations in this little volume are all my own, but the original texts are taken from *Y Caniedydd* (Abertawe: Undeb yr Annibynwyr, 1960), with kind permission, and from *Caneuon Ffydd* (2001), whose publishers, Pwyllgor Y Llyfr Emynau Cydenwadol, are not, to the best of my knowledge, still extant. I am also grateful to Seren Books for permission to print four lines from 'Cathedral Builders'.

Playlist of Selected Hymns